STRANGE NIGHTS

Strange Nights

A collection of rhyming poems and haikus

SAMUEL S. KAUFMAN

Adelaide Books
New York / Lisbon
2018

STRANGE NIGHTS
a collection of rhyming poems, and haikus
by Samuel S, Kaufman

Copyright © 2018 by Sam Kaufman

Cover design © 2018 Adelaide Books

Published by Adelaide Books, New York / Lisbon
adelaidebooks.org

Editor-in-Chief
Stevan V. Nikolic

All rights reserved. No part of this book may be reproduced in any manner whatsoever without written permission from the author except in the case of brief quotations embodied in critical articles and reviews.

For any information, please address Adelaide Books
at info@adelaidebooks.org
or write to:
Adelaide Books
244 Fifth Ave. Suite D27
New York, NY, 10001

ISBN13: 978-1-949180-19-0
ISBN10: 1-949180-19-0

Printed in the United States of America

for Steve Kaufman

Contents

Opening *10*

The Bug on the Wall *12*

Amy *14*

Maybe in America *17*

The Madhouse Cry *18*

A Haiku on Reality *21*

I Need My Heaven *22*

War *24*

Hindsight 20/20 *27*

A Haiku on Fear *29*

Soul Body Mind *30*

Miss the Violence *33*

Let's be holy *35*

A Haiku on Pop Stars *37*

You Are Not Perfect *38*

A Letter to Jimmy *40*
The Road Ahead *43*
If God *44*
A Haiku on Intelligence *47*
Chant *48*
Saint Peter *50*
Toy Soldiers *53*
A Haiku on Mistakes *55*
America the Lonely *56*
Speechless *59*
A Haiku on Love *61*
Mystic Nothing *62*
Trendy Misery *65*
A Haiku on Will *67*
Why Can't We Be Friends? *69*
PTSD (Adam's Poem) *70*
A Haiku on Loneliness *73*
Evil can be Evil *74*
A Haiku on Teenagers *77*
Those People *78*
Mad Bomb 3020 *80*
A Haiku on Nerds *83*
A Haiku on the crooked smile *85*

The Give and Take   *87*

The Perfect Life   *89*

A Haiku on Running Away   *91*

Thoughts on Hate   *92*

A Haiku on Death   *97*

No One's talking about you   *98*

A Haiku on the Dark   *101*

True God   *102*

A Haiku on Creativity   *105*

Oh Metaphor   *106*

A Haiku on Talking   *109*

Anarchist Prayer   *111*

A Haiku on Politics   *113*

Sentimental Material   *114*

My Belief   *116*

A Haiku on Small Talk   *119*

A Haiku on Good Intentions   *121*

The Scars Will Fade   *123*

About the Author   *124*

Samuel S. Kaufman

Opening

A world connected by flash drives and parallel minds
Where the stars are light years away but I can still call them mine
I see Jupiter in my dreams and Saturn in my heart
With future generations seeing the earth as the start
A black hole that takes up time and space
That explodes into fire to resemble your face
Every day feels like summer in the heart of June
My soul is like the radio with rock n roll tunes
The beat of the drum slowly progressing the wave
Taking over the old leaving a new life to pave
The cities are like tomb stones blocking the path
Making the symbol of another perfect epitaph
The priest starts the sermon in memory of the past
The people sit in pews feeling angelic at last
The people stand up and shout with vigorous praise
For the ones who dance on fiery coals without feeling the pain
These are the ones that will lead us beyond
So we move as they move and sing along to their songs
We bury the old in the dirt six feet deep
As the irrelevant politicians openly weep
The world they had made has become no more
And their words become antiques in local general stores
Where we will view them as we buy our two dollar milk
Laughing at the misguided world they had built
We did it
We did it
We got through the lies
We did it
We did it
We found the one holy eye
That saw the future as well as the past
And the peace that will finally last
We did it
We did it
We won the intellectual war
We did it
We did it
We found the wings needed to soar
Realizing the irony they had had been there from the start
We did it
We did it
We opened our hearts

Samuel S. Kaufman

The Bug on the Wall

STRANGE NIGHTS

"I shall never cry"
She said between sips of her wine
"I shall never shout"
She exclaimed in a voice riddled in doubt
You see I live a life above you all
For I live as a bug on the edge of the wall
Just waiting for the crumbs to gently fall then
WHOOSEH
You will see me crawl
To the edge of the floor in a blink of an eye
Gathering substance and hope for a fleeting supply
Leaving no time to think
How'd she get inside?
The truth is I was always there
Just a bug on the wall with her judgmental stare
Taking small bits of love in times of despair
Just dreaming of the day that you'd finally care
But as you know that day never came
As the bug on the wall was drowned in the rain
And I can't speak for you but I was never the same
Knowing my place on the wall was forever detained
I tell you this as I swallow my pride
And I take back oaths not to shout and to cry
Because it's hard to look forward
When you can still see behind
And I can't help but think how you were almost mine

Samuel S. Kaufman

Amy

STRANGE NIGHTS

Don't waste your time trying to convince me of your pain
For no one expected you to stay fully the same
We just wanted the one that made us laugh
Not this self-serving beast that's afraid of her past
Now it's true I've never told a joke in my life
Yet I still think my views are pretty precise
You don't want to be judged yet you feel it's your right
To create a world that is just so strangely polite
But I think you and I know what is obscene
And obscene doesn't live in glamor magazines
It lives with the one that's in your heart
And sadly it feels you are drifting apart
Now it's true I can be a dimwitted man
But I see what I see and I can understand
The pressures that come with being in demand
But it doesn't excuse the harm to your fans
We really are happy for your success
We just can't say the same for all of the rest
You alienated the ones that loved you most
I dred the day you become another talk show host

Samuel S. Kaufman

Maybe in America

Maybe in America
The blood doesn't bleed as red
Maybe in America
You have freedom before you are dead
Maybe in America
You're born with a way to cope
Maybe in America
You're born with a sense of hope

Samuel S. Kaufman

The Madhouse Cry

STRANGE NIGHTS

There is 1.5 gallons of blood flowing through our arms
And every day we get nicked by the cold hearted animal farm
Who laughs at the pain ca ca cawing like the crow
With the sudden shock and dismay of stubbing one's toe
On the concrete steps of the institution called life
Revolving doors of madhouses named perfect insight
The mental state of our being questioned each day
As we are kept for two weeks before being thrown out in the haze
The air so thick you could cut it with a blade
And feed it to your children as the substance they crave
Slowly poisoning the mind that comprehends social cues
Being mistaken for Christians Muslims or Jews
Not understanding which way leads to the light
We burn bibles the Koran and the Torah out of spite
Feeling we have been cheated out of finding the correct path
While the so called leaders just sit stare on their ass
Twiddling their thumbs singing their spiritual lullabies
That drown out the sound of the madhouse cry
And turn a cold shoulder to all who are inside
'Eli, Eli, lama sabachthani?'
'My God, My God, why have you forsaken me?
Why is this the only thing Jesus said I find true?
There is 1.5 gallons of blood flowing through my body
And I don't know for who

Samuel S. Kaufman

A Haiku on Reality

No more suffering?
No more misunderstood pain?
You sir are insane

Samuel S. Kaufman

I Need My Heaven

STRANGE NIGHTS

I don't believe in mercy
Or where it goes

I don't believe in the father son
Or the Holy Ghost

My back's against the wall
That crumbles at my weight

I want to find my heaven
I don't care how long it takes

I just want to be free
No amazing grace just a new opportunity
I want peace and love as far as the eye can see
But I know I won't love heaven if you're not there with me

Because there's a dark side to every light
And for every priest there's a sinner who won't put up a fight

But as I see the signs that lead to the pride and true
I know there can be no heaven without you

Can we do as we promised and search every inch of the sea
And forget about all of our mental instabilities?
Can we be the ones we were always meant to be?
And can you see a heaven without me?

Samuel S. Kaufman

War

STRANGE NIGHTS

My heart, cries for all who have died
The ones who are in hiding
And the ones who survived
My heart beats even if it's empty inside

Death, is only part of the dream
And only the scholars of war truly know what that means
But you can't hold together what's breaking apart at the seams
And not even the shot of a gun can fully muffle the screams

Peace, is such a simple thought
But they complicate the issue like they're tangled in knots
They don't care about their people or the ones they have fought
Their souls are like peaches that were left out to rot

I feel, and I know you do too
Let's not fight another battle that we're just meant to lose
Let's take all our weapons and break them in two
Let's take white flags and help bandage all wounds

Samuel S. Kaufman

Hindsight 20/20

Keep with the hearts that keep you alive
As you ride the stallion through the sinister gates
Let light shine on those who are wicked
So they may bask in their own disgrace
Create cities upon mounds of dirt
And build churches in thy name
Let your creatures live the lives they choose
And let not one be ashamed
Take the love you find within
And create landmarks in its grace
Make your guns shoot out roses
And find peace at one's own pace
Promise this to me as I give you my final breath
For I have found the clear perspective
That only comes with death

Samuel S. Kaufman

A Haiku on Fear

My fear of death is
Just a construct of my real
Fear that is to live

Samuel S. Kaufman

Soul Body Mind

STRANGE NIGHTS

Body mind and soul!
Body mind and soul!
Financial security from money thrown in a hole
Black cats broken mirrors and not one house has been sold
Please tell me why has it gotten so cold?
The air in my apartment has been broken for months
I won't swallow my pride therefore I have had no lunch
I'm starving
I'm shaking
My bones won't stop aching
I am a car on a highway that's run out of gas
As other cars won't stop they just stare as they pass
Selfish I say as I pull to the side
The sun beats on my neck and I have no place to hide
And after all of this pain people still say I whine
They think cause they got through it should be easy for me
But they forget the pain of this broken industry
They forgot how to manage heat without lighting a coal
And have lost sight of their body mind and soul

Samuel S. Kaufman

STRANGE NIGHTS

Miss the Violence

You miss the violence
And you miss the pain
When the room that's full of silence
Matches your empty brain

Samuel S. Kaufman

Let's be holy

Holy love
Oh praise the saints in the skies above
Holy truth
Love is pain when you're in your youth
Oh sing me straight sing me a song
And pray I learn to sing along
Holy holy holy you
Holy love and holy truth
Let light guide me through the sea
Because you're only holy when you're free

Samuel S. Kaufman

A Haiku on Pop Stars

Laziness in art
Is a sin they will give you
A million bucks for

Samuel S. Kaufman

You Are Not Perfect

You are not perfect
I'm sorry I cannot lie
You will never be perfect
No matter how hard you try
Everyone is killing themselves to be perfect
And I don't know why
You covet the look of the ones on the magazine
Then write blogs on your hatred of their personalities
Turns out perfection leads to mild hypocrisy
You are not perfect
I'm sorry but this is real
You will never be perfect
No matter how they tell you to feel
Never let anyone tell you you're perfect
You always need to strive for more
If you believe you are perfect you will forget what you're fighting for
And what you're fighting for is equality in self
For that is not perfection it's just basic mental health
You need to ignore the songs that tell you you're the best
Because in reality you are just like the rest
But so am I!
Trust me this is a reason to rejoice
Because you cannot have perfection and a unique voice
My body looks like a child's misshapen clay
And this is something that haunts me each and every single day
But I know I can change and that's what gets me along
To say I'm perfect now would just be perfectly wrong
And I don't want to die just sitting on the couch
To be perfect is to be complacent without the instinct of doubt
And you have to doubt yourself
It gives you the fear to survive
We are imperfect beings
Not angels yet to die
You are not perfect
I'm not sorry anymore
You will never be perfect
But just wait for what's in store
Because striving to be perfect is how you break down the doors
And find the part of yourself that is always trying to be more

Samuel S. Kaufman

A Letter to Jimmy

STRANGE NIGHTS

Stop laughing you corporate pawn!
Yes we need substance not just celebrities singing songs
It's people like you that let me know I'll never see fame
On the bright side I won't have to play your stupid board games
My god man you are the death of art
With the maturity of a 4th grader laughing at a fart
Hey at least when they do it its natural
You're like what a robot thinks is casual
You are half a man sitting with your suit and tie
I'd say hang yourself with it but I'm afraid I'd still hear your "laugh" as you die
Did you see I put laughs in quotations?
That's because it's as fake your impersonations
But hey celebrities love that "laugh"
But maybe they're just surprised you can do it with your lips sewn to their ass
Now I know your probably thinking I'm being too harsh
But man am I getting pleasure from tearing you apart
You are by far the worst thing on TV
And yes that includes the shows that call themselves reality

Samuel S. Kaufman

The Road Ahead

I'm going mad
Well I'm going ballistic
And even my doctor has run out of prescriptions
Oh can't you relate to this lack of interest?
Oh can't you relate to this mental illness?
The most important thing in life is to get on through
Even if those demons keep following you
You can never out run them oh can't you see?
That's why I let them walk right next to me
We sometimes have chats about the pains of the past
They try to drag me down but I just walk and I laugh
Why would I let anything drag me down?
The road ahead looks so clear to me now

Samuel S. Kaufman

If God

STRANGE NIGHTS

If god knew my name my name would be peace
And he would introduce me to every single person he meets

If god knew my name my name would be love
And I'd be inside your soul and would circulate through your blood

If god knew my name my name would be hope
And he would cast out my image to all who must cope

The darkest hour is always a minute way
And it's hard to hunt when you always feel like the prey
You find yourself choking on the thickness of air
And it comes far too easy to say that no one cares

But if you learn how to smile you can learn how to breathe
And the acceptance of other is a thing you won't need
Because life runs in circles that can tire the brain
Leaving everyone around you to say you're insane

But you must ignore these people they are tired and weak
And you should never acknowledge how the ignorant think
Because doubtful minds search for self-conscious brains
All to convince you that god doesn't know your name

Samuel S. Kaufman

A Haiku on Intelligence

There is a genius
That lies in each and every
Idiot on earth

Samuel S. Kaufman

Chant

Killer madness full of gladness
Don't worry children you're alone

Morning glory allegory
Can't break my words with sticks and stones

Mother father sister brother
We've lost love between one another

Water fire get me higher
Don't believe everything you hear from the choir

Chant chant chant
From this high you all look like ants

Chant chant chant
I no longer feel stupid in the heart of dance

I've thrown my manifestos in the lake
For fear only the fish would partake
In the deepest thoughts within my mind
For the fish know indifference is not a crime

Chant chant chant
I can't help but laugh at the tightness of my pants

I keep gaining weight at every injustice I see
And at this point I've become morbidly obese
I can only lose weight if I stop watching the 5 o clock news
But I've become too complacent in the blues

So I won't look away I just can't
All I want to do is

Chant Chant Chant

Samuel S. Kaufman

Saint Peter

STRANGE NIGHTS

Oh Saint Peter
I see you in my dreams
From this I have interpreted
It is guidance that I need
Oh Saint Peter
Please tell me if I'll ever find my way
In a world full of liars and silent decay
Do you believe I have the strength to move on?
Even if all my interest is gone
Oh Saint Peter
Your face looks so soft in my dream
Oh Saint Peter
You know just what this means
You are telling me something I can't tell myself
But Oh Saint Peter
I never asked for your help
I don't need to see you every night in my dreams
And yet you appear
And that's what is comforting me

Samuel S. Kaufman

Toy Soldiers

We are all toy soldiers fighting the war of "LIFE"
Fighting for our "RIGHTS"
We are all toy soldiers fighting the war of "PEACE"
Toy soldiers fighting for our "BELIEFS"

Samuel S. Kaufman

STRANGE NIGHTS

A Haiku on Mistakes

There's a nice clear night
That paves its way into the
Bright fires of hell

Samuel S. Kaufman

America the Lonely

STRANGE NIGHTS

My ode sweet true to you America
My ode to the land that's falling apart
I sing to you the white and blue
Destruction always was the one true art

Oh my holy land where did you go?
Where is the hope and the dreams that we know?
I expect an answer within the hour
this is what I expect from the nation of power

Oh Why can't you stop seeing peace as a means to an end?
And when will the magic truly begin?
The question I give to you
The know it all nation that's great at lighting the fuse

Save me now oh king of the sea
Stop hurting the ones that are just like me

Samuel S. Kaufman

Speechless

Yes to the living
And
No to the dead
Happy thoughts beginning
Leaving nothing else
To be said

Samuel S. Kaufman

STRANGE NIGHTS

A Haiku on Love

Love is all you need
The most important sentence
That was ever said

Samuel S. Kaufman

Mystic Nothing

STRANGE NIGHTS

Mystic vibrations in the word of love
Yet not as sophisticated as smoking bud
Or as simple as just pulling the pud
It just stands to be the idiotic mind set of simple conversations
And the exaggerated worth of useless situations

I can see through walls yet I'm going blind
Oh Satan you've really done it this time

I can't think about what I am
Only what I'm not
I'm looking for solidarity with the people who were shot

The gods have given me the ability to speak my mind
Unfortunately they gave everyone the ability to ignore people who whine
There must be some other way to settle this matter
I lose at least one masterpiece every hour

I have broken the fine china and drank all the beer
But I promise there is still room in my heart for you my dear
Just let me push my self-respect out
And you can nuzzle yourself amongst all my doubt

I love you all, more than you can see
Just don't quote me on that because image is key
No one ever got famous just preaching love
Well some did but I think all their work is crud

Trendy Misery

Thank god misery became trendy
Without it I wouldn't be attractive
Thank god misery became a trend
It's made everyone so reactive
Everyone looks for love
Just like they know they should
Thank god misery became a trend
Because now my odds are pretty good

Samuel S. Kaufman

STRANGE NIGHTS

A Haiku on Will

I've lost all my will
It's the most freeing thing you
Can do with yourself

Samuel S. Kaufman

STRANGE NIGHTS

Why Can't We Be Friends?

When the sheep befriends the wolf
And the cat befriends the mouse
Is when man befriends his enemy
And puts back together his house

Samuel S. Kaufman

PTSD
(Adam's Poem)

STRANGE NIGHTS

I once knew a man who fought for his life
From the moment he woke up to the end of the night
A casualty of war and an endless fight
Memories of pain that clouded his sight

Every day was like walking in mud
And he could still hear the screams from his friends up above
They shouted for answers and cried out for truth
Leading the man to start tying the noose

As he tied he thought of his life
But all he got were explosions and people wielding their knives
He managed two tears before kicking the chair
Now a hanging symbol on how life's not fair

His parents cried at the loss of their child
And his wife's whole world went black for a while
His friends felt lost by the holes in their heart
And everyone's heart felt like it had been torn apart

The moral of the story is that war is hell
And it can make you do terrible things to yourself
We must treat our veterans with the best of care
Because some day you can look and they won't be there

Samuel S. Kaufman

STRANGE NIGHTS

A Haiku on Loneliness

The harmonica
Has become my new lover
And I blow just fine

Samuel S. Kaufman

Evil can be Evil

STRANGE NIGHTS

Can you have both redemption and vengeance?
I don't think you can
I don't think you can trick fate at any sleight of hand
For there is a master that controls us all
Call it god call it fate
There's something there that knows the difference between charisma and hate
One that sees with the one true eye
As we are ignorant to the television planets falling from the sky
They're about to crush us are you mad!?
The only reality I see is on TV my god how sad
Cursing your generation has become such a casual thing
But I'm a hipster at heart so please god just kill me
I can't keep pouring out my soul just to make a buck
Since I've been sober I've become jaded as fuck
I've run out of anything decent to say
I have a library full of words all on an empty page
But the real problem is not what's going on with my mind
Or from the lack of interest in which it finds
No
It's about the world that is constantly turning
And about a country that can convince itself that it's not burning
We are people in dire need of salvation
For the evil brought through unnatural insemination
There is hate in the heart of every man woman and child
With madness and sexual impulses running wild
I just ask to please stop the hate
Or at the very least learn to tolerate
You have to stop blaming others for all of your pain
And stop seeing redemption and vengeance as one and the same

Samuel S. Kaufman

A Haiku on Teenagers

Child if you must cut
Cut the papers that have torn
Your soul into shreds

Samuel S. Kaufman

Those People

I've seen how fast a man can run
Through 20 cycles of the sun
I've seen the work of life invaders
That move through the swamps like alligators
To devour thoughts inside your mind
And break the spirit of once divine
It makes you less open to help
And ignore the heart within yourself

These people
These people are always in a position of power
And can make the clock mock you after every hour
They crash your fragile mental state
Then use your time to liquidate

These bastards
These bastards don't think of you as a person
Therefore they don't recognize their mental incursion
They just pick and pick and pick and pick
Until every day you wake up sick

Sick of the time you devout to these monsters
Sick of the mirror that only shows an imposter
Of a man that was once filled with hope
Who won't even reach to the bottle to cope
He just digs through what's left us his soul
To remember the inspirational quotes he was told

"It's always darkest before the dawn"
No that won't work I'm too far gone
"You can't love someone else until you love yourself"
No doesn't work for me or my mental health
"Happiness is a road travelled not a destination"
Yes! That will work because it makes sense of my creation

Maybe someday I'll look back and it won't that bad
And when I think of the monsters I won't feel depressed or mad
I just know it was a part of my life
And despite it all I put up one hell of a fight

But as for now I still have to go to work in the morning
And do my time for a weekly earning
But tomorrow I might just express a little attitude
Because when you fight back those people just don't know what to do

Samuel S. Kaufman

Mad Bomb 3020

Life invaders
Disenfranchised masturbators
Sucking the tit of the last man's wish

They break the world that will soon be gone
Broken souls walking in the living mad bomb
Destroying each other with both fire and hate
They've reached a new level where pain doesn't discriminate

It finds a place in all of our hearts
And they find solace in tearing each other apart
Now we've seen how far a man can sink
Once fully immersed in primal instinct

I see orgies flooding the streets at night
But I'm too timid to go so I just sit and I write
About all the things that I see
With a little artistic twist covered in self-loathing envy

Why can't I hurt people too?
It's not my strong morals because I really want to
My brain fantasizes about killing just like everyone else
And I'm no better than them because I don't even run out to help

It's a new world they decided to create
But I'm just a coward too afraid to partake
God was proven to be a myth years ago
Yet I here I am on my knees praying for hope

Lord help me become one with the crowd
Let me walk with the mob with my head held proud
Let me move toward the fire just like the moth
Keep my head held high before they cut it off

Samuel S. Kaufman

STRANGE NIGHTS

A Haiku on Nerds

I remember when
Being a nerd was seen as
Social suicide

Samuel S. Kaufman

A Haiku on the crooked smile

Carry on my child.
Live like the pretentious who,
Got lost in the smile

Samuel S. Kaufman

The Give and Take

If you take me now

I'll give you my love

Because I am poor

But my love is enough

So please believe in the give and take

Because I believe in futures

But I refuse to wait

Samuel S. Kaufman

STRANGE NIGHTS

The Perfect Life

You impressive man
You have it all but you don't understand
That if she loves you
You have everything you need
If she loves you
You are the luckiest soul I have seen
And she does love you
In day and in dream
Please promise to see the light in which that brings
Please tell me it brings you joy in the night
Because she loves you
And you have the perfect life

Samuel S. Kaufman

STRANGE NIGHTS

A Haiku on Running Away

The sympathetic
Angel rides away in the
Moaning bright midnight

Samuel S. Kaufman

Thoughts on Hate

STRANGE NIGHTS

This poem will become famous I'm sure of it
Because in this poem I will show you all my hate
A catastrophic symphony so beautiful I am forced to write as it dictates

The world is a black void of pointless moments
I am reminded every time I go to work
I see the boss control the people
All on an 8.50 perk
They come back every day just to ignore the harm
Me? I would rather starve
I see this because I have to
They don't because it's what they choose
I am self-aware to a fault
And at the end we both lose

I don't have many friends
Or was that obvious?
I don't care anymore
The ones who care are just like me
And what would you want that for?
A sarcastic asshole a good friend does not make
You don't want an egotistic loser that's only full of hate

I have always said self-awareness is a curse
Because it is bestowed upon the lazy
For every time I start to change my vision just gets hazy
Even though I see my faults with perfect clarity
I only feed the mess
Writing poems such as these with no answer to my distress

Samuel S. Kaufman

I am breaking inside but the glue's across the room
I won't get up because there seems to be a comfort to my gloom
I see some tape beside me
That should get me through the day
It comes off every time I shower
But lately that's ok

I smoke cigarettes as I write
It may be the only thing that I love
You don't have to like someone to love them
And that's why love isn't enough
Love is crying at a murder trial
Safely from the stands
But love is not enough to defend yet another guilty man

I am drowning and my life preserver is writing
But this is not a journal and I need money for what I'm inciting
You can call me a sell out
But all my unpublished works could fill up Nebraska
From lack of luck and paper cuts
The blood flows all the way to Alaska
You see my love is meant to hurt you
Then nurse you back to health
But sadly I'm just hurting you
And for that I hurt myself

I'm disgusted by my masturbation
And I'm disgusted people won't admit they are to
People like to believe they don't watch porn before work
Although I know they do
The whole worlds masturbating and to deny that is stunning
You think people would know by now
The world becomes clear as you're cumming
If I could make my decisions as I came we would have peace within the hour
But I always make them after I cum
When the regret has taken power

STRANGE NIGHTS

But sex is normal and should never take the blame
It's not sex's fault the world makes decisions
Like it just came

Everyone's to opinionated
There's too many outlets not to be
He said while writing this poem
Oh the irony
I've had too many disagreements while on the internet
Where we just feed our egos
And take the confidence we can get
The fact that we can do this insulting to the dirt
Because I relate too much to these people
And oh my God that hurts

I just wish I could make people laugh
I always indulge my itch to try
But I exacerbate those around me
Who would clearly rather die
But when I get a laugh it's like heroin
The opium of success
But you won't love a joke if you hate the comedian
And so I am under constant distress

Too much hate will kill you
But enough can inspire change
Too much hate will blind you
But a world without it would be strange
I have a hate for my failure
And a hate that wants to give
This is why I write
And this is why I live

Samuel S. Kaufman

STRANGE NIGHTS

A Haiku on Death

The sweet song of death
Is sung by the angels in
The times most forgot

Samuel S. Kaufman

No One's talking about you

STRANGE NIGHTS

Ever get the feeling they're talking about you?
When you know it's such a silly thing to do
There's over a billon words out there
And not one reason you should care
Yet you can't help but think they're talking about you
They're probably just talking about the fun they had years ago
And you're just self-aware enough to know
That it's just your insecurities
And there's no reason you can see
Why they'd be talking about you
You're just wishing they would go away
Then you wouldn't think about what they have to say
But what I'm about to tell you is the truth
I promise they're not talking about you

STRANGE NIGHTS

A Haiku on the Dark

I've found that the dark
Is always more appealing
Than the brightest light

Samuel S. Kaufman

True God

STRANGE NIGHTS

Debutantes and masquerades
A bastard child a runway
You are here you are heard
You are the black sheep of this herd
A constant thorn in potent side
You're Malcom X you're Jesus Christ
I wait for you beside the door
Down on my knees till they get sore
With hopes of salvation on its way
I think I've lost my chance to pray
See God hates the love for an idol
But it was you who were there when I was suicidal
Not a faceless shape or a deep repent
Nor judgment based on malcontent
No
It was only you that understood
You have to see the face beneath the hood
And search the brain for the peace inside
Because with you my peace could never hide
And even though you're not with me every day
I have the songs you used to play
And I am reminded with every chord
Sometimes god is not the lord

Samuel S. Kaufman

STRANGE NIGHTS

A Haiku on Creativity

I've gained this illness
That makes me happier than
The days that I'm well

Samuel S. Kaufman

Oh Metaphor

STRANGE NIGHTS

Loose change sticks to my naked body as I sleep at night
As they fall I dig for the quarters with the sun through the curtains too bright
I only find Pennies
Shit
Oh metaphor oh metaphor please describe my life
Please find my pain artistic with clever insight
Please give me a reason to continue this despair
All for the audience that isn't even there
Every woman loves a good basket case
At least that's what I tell myself when I picture your face
Oh metaphor oh metaphor you're getting too real for me now
How can I continue when I can't see the crowd?
How am I expected to keep up my boyish charm?
Without the full embrace of insanity and bodily harm
I promise everything I do I do for you
I tell myself in the mirror every day just to get through
Another pointless day doing what I'm told
Oh metaphor oh metaphor
This is growing too old

Samuel S. Kaufman

A Haiku on Talking

A mouthful of shit
Is a livable aliment
Until you swallow

Samuel S. Kaufman

STRANGE NIGHTS

Anarchist Prayer

The first step to change is rejection
The second step is to abandon all ideas of perfection
The third is to take down all the center fools
Because change can only come from a rejection of all rules

Samuel S. Kaufman

STRANGE NIGHTS

A Haiku on Politics

Too many Satan's
Is either a good band name
Or it's just congress

Samuel S. Kaufman

Sentimental Material

STRANGE NIGHTS

Where is the sweatshirt I gave you years before?
Buried in piles of ash deep on your bedroom floor?
Of course you know I'm just using ash as a metaphor
Because generally speaking it's not fair to call you a whore
And saying something doesn't quite make it true
But make no mistake there's something wrong about you
There's something wrong with how you choose to view love
You see it as pity handed from above
You think it can cleanse you of all of your sins
My god is anyone allowed to be genuine?
Is anyone allowed to tell you what they think?
I will because the memories have brought me to the brink
Not a week goes by I don't think of the pain
That you selfishly caused me in unusual ways
The times of gold that you turned into shit
I wish I could take the advice of my folks and get over it
But I can't because I'm lost in the thought
That somewhere you're smiling without your stomach in knots
That every day goes by and you don't think of me at all
And I'm just a bitter man that never got a call
Do you know how many poems I've written about this?
It's hard to find new synonyms for anger and piss
It's hard to justify my anger anymore
But I can't let it die
Because I can still feel the sores
And I can still picture my sweatshirt
Buried in ash on your bedroom floor

Samuel S. Kaufman

My Belief

STRANGE NIGHTS

If everything we do has a purpose
Then why does it feel as though the good lord has cursed us?
Why does it seem like we're walking through hell?
And why are the questions always pointed at myself?
If I had an answer I'm sure it would stop
But the point of the hike's not always to get to the top
Sometimes it's just about the air around your head
A time to let in life
Rather than focus on death
My friends we live for the hikes
The moments of joy and the killing of spite
In search of joy morning through night
This I think is the meaning of life

Samuel S. Kaufman

STRANGE NIGHTS

A Haiku on Small Talk

Sick bastards roaming
Finding sanctuary in
Lost conversations

Samuel S. Kaufman

STRANGE NIGHTS

A Haiku on Good Intentions

The blood on your hands
Can only truly be cleansed
With good intentions

Samuel S. Kaufman

The Scars Will Fade

All scars fade with time
No matter how deep you cut
The clock may tease you now
But I promise you're in luck
Because the next day always comes too soon
Then you can look back and laugh
Because time heals all wounds

Samuel S. Kaufman

About the Author

Samuel S. Kaufman is a poet from Asheville, North Carolina. Samuel has been described as a "Punk Rock Poet" due to his writing often showing the rebellious spirit that lives in punk rock music. Samuel's influences in writing are writers from the "Beat Generation". Writers such as Allen Ginsberg, Jack Kerouac, and William S. Burroughs. He also gained much of his love for poetry from poets such as Charles Bukowski, Billy Collins, and Sylvia Plath. As well as being a published poet Samuel is also an accomplished songwriter. He plays six instruments and is constantly putting new music out online, as well as playing live shows all around his local town. The connection of music and poetry is important to Samuel as he often records spoken word poetry with a backdrop of music he plays himself. You can acquire Samuel's music at:
bandcamp.com/samuelkaufman.
Samuel believes that poetry has the power to change lives, and so he spends every day trying to write something worthy of that power.

www.ingramcontent.com/pod-product-compliance
Lightning Source LLC
Chambersburg PA
CBHW030120100526
44591CB00009B/471